11/23

To April - a woman
who has helped me more than
She knows - Mike & I hope
You enjoy what's on these pages as much as
we enjoyed making the memories!

Love, Christella-Kurz

Captivating Coastal Creatures of Southwest Florida

Christine J. Relli-Kunz

Halo
PUBLISHING
INTERNATIONAL

ISBN: 978-1-63765-251-0
LCCN: 2022908870

Halo Publishing International, LLC
www.halopublishing.com

Printed and bound in the United States of America

This book was made possible because of my dear aunt Peggy Greshik. In 2015, I put together thirty small photo albums of fish, shorebirds, and other marine-related nature photos, with a little blurb about each picture. Fondly referring to it as my Fishmas Book, I included one with each Christmas card.

After Aunt Peggy opened her card and saw the Fishmas Book, she immediately called me and quite seriously exclaimed, "You should publish this as a children's book!"

While I appreciated her praise, I just laughed off her comments, as my intent was just to share Mike's and my fishing experiences with family and friends. But in the years since then, there have been numerous occasions when other recipients of the Fishmas Book have voiced the same opinion, not to mention Aunt Peggy's persistent urging that I actually write a book.

My greatest recognition goes to my husband, Michael Kunz, for his constant support and encouragement. He never complained about the countless hours I spent on this book. Before I met Mike, I barely had the slightest attraction to, or appreciation of, marine life and nature in general. But once we started dating, Mike began piquing that interest in me, cultivating and nurturing it into a passionate awe of the incredible nature that surrounds us. Besides being the best husband ever, Mike is also the most competent fishing guide one could ask for and my personal tour guide wherever we go. He has a knack for seeing things that I normally overlook. Mike has given me a gift you can't wrap because it is too big—it has enriched my life to a level I never dreamed of.

I also extend my heartfelt gratitude to my coworkers at Yarnell & Peterson, P.A. and to my friends and family who have helped me get past my occasional writer's block and have provided invaluable opinions and guidance that only adults who have raised children can give. Because Mike and I have no children, they helped me to see the world through children's eyes.

CONTENTS

INTRODUCTION

Shortly after Mike and I started dating in 1992, we bought a ten-foot johnboat and a small trolling motor that we loaded into his Dodge Caravan and hauled anywhere from Port of the Islands to Lovers Key State Park almost every weekend. We eventually graduated to a twelve-foot and then a fourteen-foot johnboat. In 2001, we bought a sixteen-foot Hewes Bayfisher flats boat, which we still use today, and expanded our horizons to Pine Island Sound and Sanibel Island.

In November of 2021, I was inexplicably overcome with an intense desire to share our photographs and experiences with others. The next thing I knew, I was writing this book. These photographs barely scratch the surface of the precious moments we have shared and scarcely capture the beauty and wonder of our aquatic environment. But I've tried my best and hope you enjoy them as much as we do.

CHRISTINE J. RELLI-KUNZ

CRANKY CRUSTACEANS

The boat ramp was pitch-black at 5:30 a.m., but for a sole light pole at end of the middle dock. Except for the gentle lapping of the tiny waves against the boat ramp, it was so quiet you could hear a pin drop. As we started to load our boat, I heard an unusual scraping noise coming from where the edge of water meets the ramp. A slight motion startled me, and the hair on the back of my neck stood up. I reached for the spotlight and aimed it in the direction of the movement. I was shocked; in the beam of light was the biggest hermit crab I had ever seen. It was the giant saltwater hermit crab pictured on the opposite page. Weighing at least five pounds, it was longer than my foot and taller than my ankle—and that was without the shell!

Also pictured on the opposite page are a couple of hermit crabs about the size we usually come across. You can see how small the second crab is, and the other crab was about as big as the palm of my hand.

Pictured above is a spider crab—creepy, isn't it?

CHRISTINE J. RELLI-KUNZ

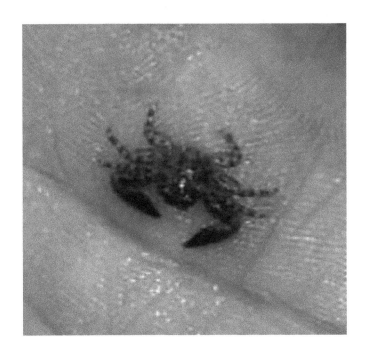

Stone crabs are considered a delicacy. They are also a critter to be feared and respected. Those claws have enough strength to crush or seriously injure a finger or toe—but they are so YUMMY! It was really entertaining to watch Mike learn how to catch and handle these crabs. But he caught on pretty quickly and is quite good at it now. I'm also happy to report we both still have all our toes and fingers!

You only eat the meat from a stone crab's claws and knuckles—the joint at the base of the claw—but it is only lawful to harvest claws that are over a certain size. Mike uses long-nosed pliers to take the crabs out of the trap; he then places them in a bowl, in order to grab them from behind, and removes any legal-sized claws. After taking its claws, the crab is released alive; over a period of time, it will grow new claws to replace those that were removed.

Above is a photo of a baby stone crab that came out of our trap. Also pictured are what stone-crab claws look like when they are cooked.

When we check our crab traps, we first motor by them to see if any tripletail—pictured later in the "Fierce Fighters" section—are hanging out under the buoys. If there are, we circle back to fish for them. Afterward, as Mike pulls each of our crab traps up from the water's depths, my anticipation mounts. Mike has to be careful as he pulls on the rope because of all the marine life attached to it. We find lots of seaweed, barnacles, crabs, urchins, and the occasional seahorse. As Mike pulls each trap on board the boat, scores of baby crabs, shrimp, snails, starfish, and urchins also fall from the outside surfaces of the trap.

Then the best part happens—Mike opens the trap by cutting the zip tie, moving aside the latches, and finally lifting the top. We never know what we'll find inside; it could be empty, or it could be filled with stone crabs. But, for me, the best catch is the bycatch or nontargeted marine species—those sea creatures unintentionally caught in the trap like other kinds of crustaceans, both occupied and empty shells, and a variety of different fish.

CHRISTINE J. RELLI-KUNZ

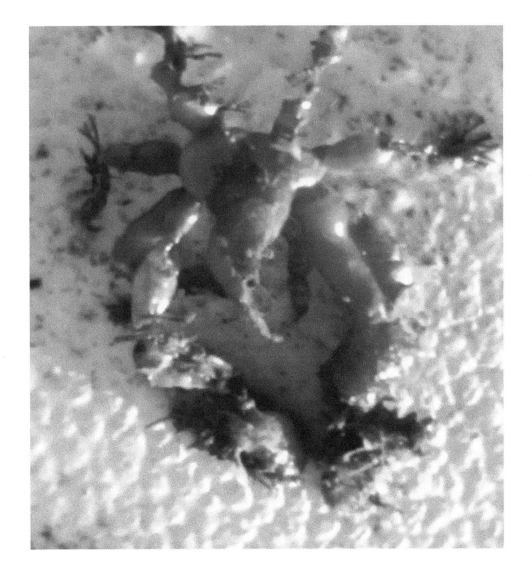

Some other crabs we commonly find in our traps or on the ropes tied to the traps are arrow crabs. The features common to the three I have pictured are the arrowhead-shaped bodies; the long, thin legs; and the long, slender, hornlike protrusion from their heads. But what is really interesting about these guys is how different they look, despite being the same species! The first crab seems almost bare, except for a few hooked bristles on its legs. The second crab has noticeably more hooked bristles that appear to have seaweed or small twigs stuck to them. The crab pictured above appears to have either orange sea sponge or soft coral adhered to its entire body. And there is definitely some unidentifiable muck stuck to its front legs. This guy's horn may be broken, but you can still see hooked bristles toward the bottom of its back legs.

The reason that all three crabs can look so different but still be the same species is that arrow crabs are part of a group of crabs known as decorator crabs. Decorator crabs use anything they can find to their liking as camouflage for protection. The more stuff they stick to their bodies, the safer they are from predators. They walk very slowly when out of the water because they have to raise their legs very high to move. Watching them is similar to watching a monster movie in slow motion! I took several short video segments of these guys walking around our deck—it was freaky!

CHRISTINE J. RELLI-KUNZ

The calico crab—top picture on opposite page—is definitely the prettiest species of crab we find in our crab traps. Their spot patterns, color, and shading are different on every crab.

The pictures immediately below the calico crab are of a common pass or swimming crab. Pass crabs float out with the tide and are great bait for just about any Southwest Florida fish species, especially tarpon, permit, pompano, redfish, black drum, and snook, all of which are pictured in later sections of this book. You can easily identify a pass crab by its back legs—they are more like paddles than legs. Swimming crabs stay fairly small; they only grow to about four times larger than the crab pictured. To catch them, we slowly cruise, with or against the outgoing tide, while scooping them up in a bait net. But you have to be quick!

What's really unusual about this particular crab, though, is its markings. Pass crabs are generally light brown with faint blotching on their shells and slightly bluish or reddish tinting on their legs. This crab was vividly splotchy and had a pigmentation flaw in its shell that resulted in the perfect white triangle shown in the picture. It's one of my favorites. Of course, there was no way I could use it for bait. Happily, I can report it was safely released to, hopefully, have many more uniquely colored babies.

Speaking of babies, the third crab pictured on the opposite page is a fouling assemblage crab. Those are the ridges in the palm of my hand on which it is sitting—that's how small this crab is! But what is so amazing about this particular crab is that, when that photograph was taken, it was old enough to be carrying eggs on its belly!

The crab pictured above is an average pass crab. It may have very well been someone's bait, which was released after not being used. I believe that to be true because it's growing brand-new claws. Just look at those little claws! Its claws should be at least as long as its other legs.

CHRISTINE J. RELLI-KUNZ

One of the most dangerous little critters we've come across is the mantis shrimp, which is pictured at the top of the opposite page. It is also known among fishermen as a "thumb splitter." The mantis shrimp species common in Southwest Florida waters is a drab light brown in color and has razor-sharp front appendages that are called "raptorial claws." Mantis shrimp found in more tropical waters are brightly colored and have what looks like a boxer's glove, instead of razors, on the end of each front appendage.

The punching action of the mantis shrimp's claws is documented as the fastest movement known in the ocean. They pack the fastest punch on Earth and are known to break aquarium glass. The more tropical mantis shrimp are able to generate a noise so loud that it can stun fish! The sound may not be very loud to us, but to a fish, that's a different story.

One thing is for sure, though—NEVER handle any of them with your bare hands! We caught the mantis shrimp pictured with a dip net as it was swimming out with the tide near Big Carlos Bridge on the south end of Fort Myers Beach. We also came across one several years earlier on the mudflats while baitfishing. At that time I didn't know what they were—but I learned fast!

Though sea urchins are not crustaceans, I've pictured the purple and spiny urchins here because we frequently find them crawling inside and all around our crab traps. The movement of their mouths is mesmerizing. Their mouths open and close by growing and shrinking in diameter. The whole mouth moves around like a human eye in the eye socket, and it retracts and protrudes. It's wild to watch!

Pictured above are views of the top and underside of a horseshoe crab. If I had barnacles stuck to the base of my tail, I'd be cranky, too!

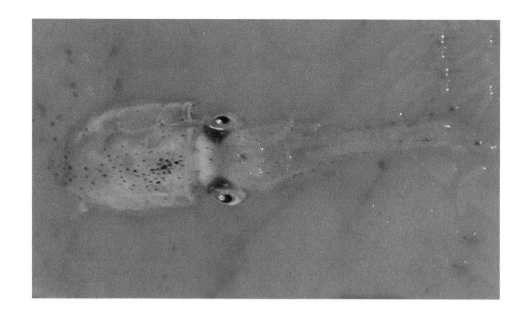

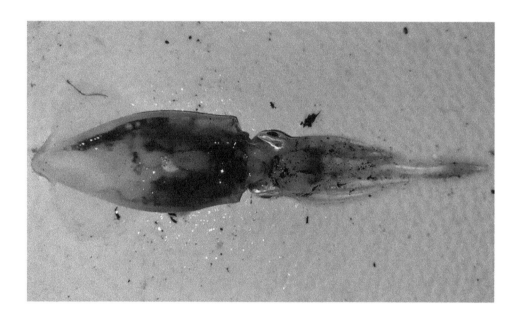

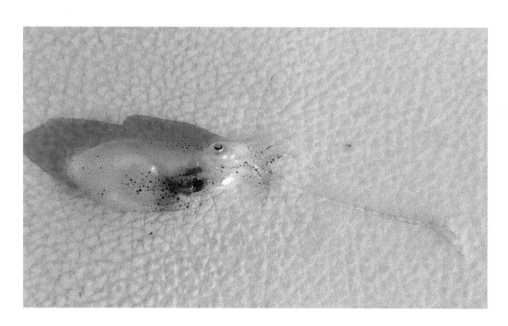

CHRISTINE J. RELLI-KUNZ

SQUISHY STUFF

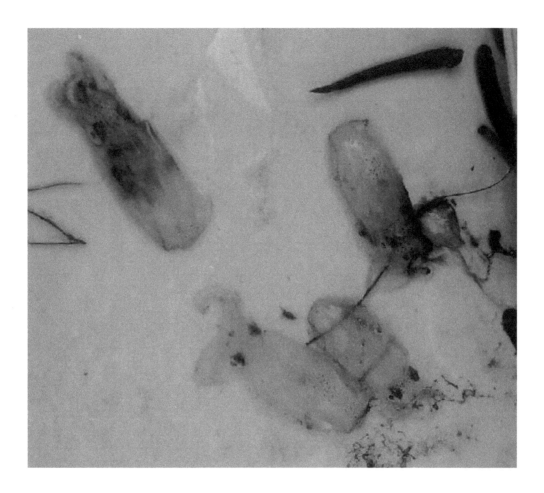

We believe the three pictures on the opposite page are of baby Atlantic squid that came out of Mike's cast net, but we're not sure about the one on the bottom. Its body shape was a little different; it had short, stumpy arms and one superlong arm with what appeared to be a sucker pad on the end. The squid-like creatures in the picture above could be squid, but it's also possible they are juvenile cuttlefish because their arms are so short. It was very dark, and they were so small that it was difficult to tell for sure. Cuttlefish are not commonly found in the Gulf of Mexico.

It's amazing to watch how fast squid can change colors. If you look closely, you can see tiny black dots in all these creatures' bodies. These dots become darker and bigger the more they are agitated. Mike has caught only a few dozen squid over the years, usually in the dark, early-morning hours, so they are hard to see when they drop out of his net.

But when Mike does get one, we know it…because they can do something else. They leak black ink everywhere on our boat! You can see from the picture above how messy they can be when they drop out of the net. Unfortunately, because of the darkness, it's easy to accidentally step on them. When we do, black ink goes everywhere!

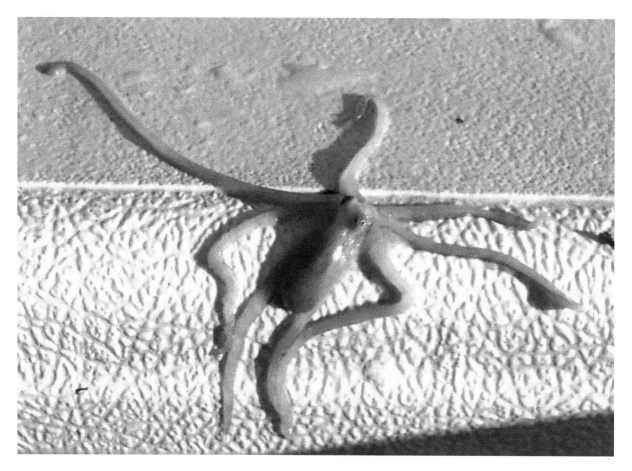

CHRISTINE J. RELLI-KUNZ

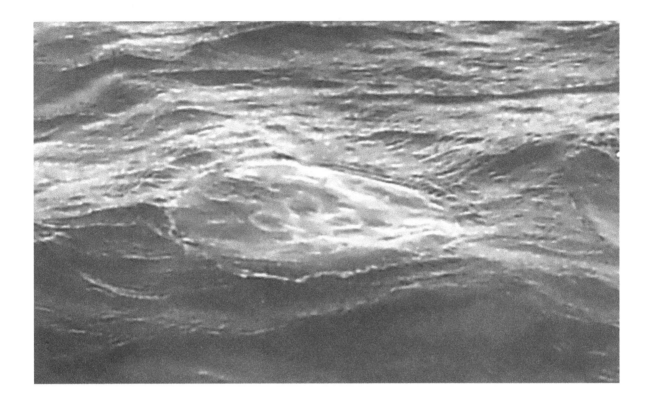

Another squishy critter we occasionally come across is the common octopus. The one pictured was caught in Mike's cast net. However, several years ago, we were about two miles offshore when we encountered hundreds, if not thousands, of baby octopi swimming or floating on the water's surface. We could have scooped up as many as we wanted in our bait net. We have no idea why that happened, nor have we seen anything like it since.

Once, Mike caught a bigger octopus, one that weighed maybe a couple of pounds, with his fishing pole! Using a five-inch mullet for bait, he was fishing for redfish above the Vanderbilt Rocks in North Naples. He felt a bite, set the hook, and reeled up an octopus. It had been hooked in one of its arms, but every time Mike attempted with his pliers to take the hook out, the octopus reached out its other tentacles to grab on to Mike's arm. After playing this game of cat and mouse for a minute or two, Mike lowered the octopus back into the water with his pole while he considered his options. He didn't want to leave the hook in the octopus.

That's when the octopus, with the hook still in one of its arms, decided to suck onto the side of our boat and crawl down to the bottom of the hull. Running out of options and still holding his fishing pole, Mike put the boat in gear and gunned the motor until the boat was on plane. The octopus finally let go of the boat, and the force of the water removed the hook from its tentacle. It was definitely one of those unique experiences!

The picture above is of a Florida moon jellyfish. They are beautiful, but they are so transparent that you need to know what to look for in order to see them. They have what appears to be a four-petaled pink flower in the middle and are edged with pink. Once when we were motoring in the Gulf of Mexico, we came across an area about the size of a football field; it was dotted with moon jellyfish every few yards. They only have a mild sting—nothing like the Portuguese man-of-war jellyfish, which, thankfully, isn't common to Southwest Florida.

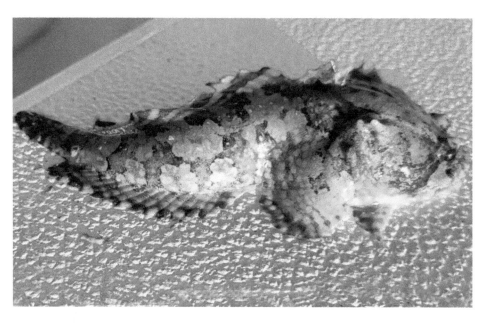

CREEPY CRITTERS

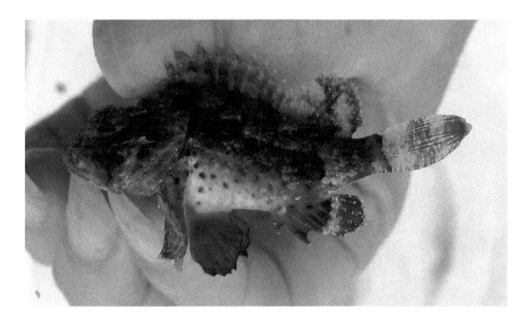

Meet the juvenile Gulf toadfish, which is pictured on the opposite page. These guys hang out on the sea bottom and are ambush feeders—you can tell because their eyes bug out of the tops of their heads. Their dorsal or top fins contain venom, so I'm very careful while I hold them. We frequently find these fish in our crab traps. While they may not be very colorful, they definitely have a variety of distinctive patterns on their bodies.

The two fish pictured above are juvenile scorpion fish. Their dorsal fins, pectoral fins on each side, and anal fins on the bottom are all filled with venom, as are the barbs on their gill plates. Divers are very careful to avoid bothering these fish. These little guys may be cute now, but when they double or even quadruple in size, watch out!

CHRISTINE J. RELLI-KUNZ

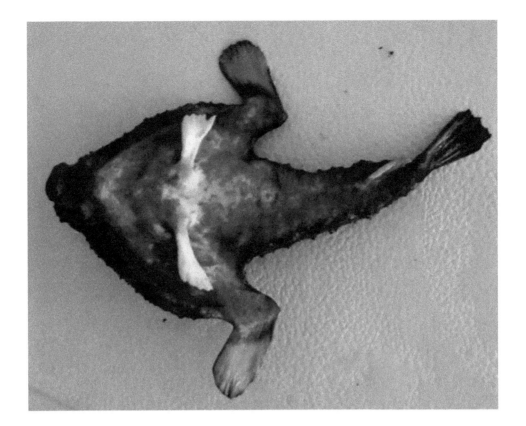

Have you ever seen a spotted batfish? Well, now you have. Weird, huh? Using their side fins more like feet than for swimming, batfish crawl along the sea bottom. Mike caught this guy in his cast net in the backwaters of Estero Bay. We've only caught two or three of these fish in the past. Check out its belly—it has white cartilage or bony appendages that act as a second pair of legs!

The fish pictured below the batfish is a remora. It uses its specially adapted head to adhere to the bottom and sides of other larger fish so it can gobble up its host's scraps, or even try to steal its food. The top of its head looks a lot like the bottom of your sneakers!

We noticed many of the redfish we caught in the fall of 2021 had remoras stuck to them. We don't recall ever seeing so many remoras on a particular species of fish before—other than on sharks, their usual hosts.

CHRISTINE J. RELLI-KUNZ

Here's one fish's mouth you DON'T want to put your fingers in—the mouth of the lizard fish pictured on the opposite page. Some teeth, huh? I used to hang chameleons on my earlobes, like earrings, when I was a kid, but I wouldn't try that with these fish! They probably got their common name from the shape of their heads and bodies. Their elongated bodies gently taper to a small tail fin. I caught this guy with my fishing pole, but Mike has caught plenty of them in his cast net, too. By the way, that is not my blood!

The fish above is a Gulf pipefish. These fish normally swim vertically, with their heads down, mimicking the sway of seagrass to conceal themselves from would-be predators and to ambush prey. Mike frequently catches these in his cast net while throwing on grass beds. To me, pipefish look and move more like snakes than fish.

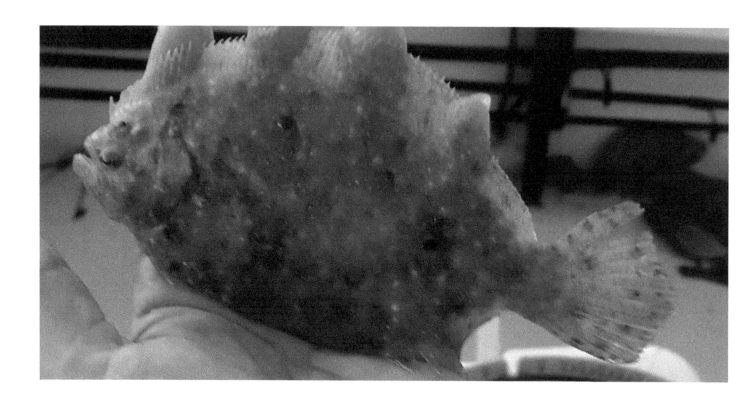

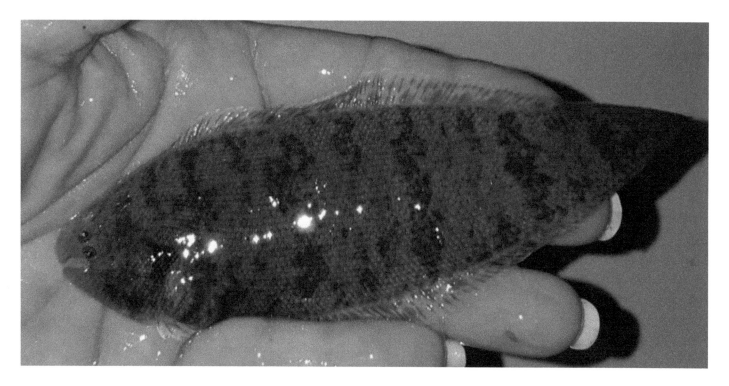

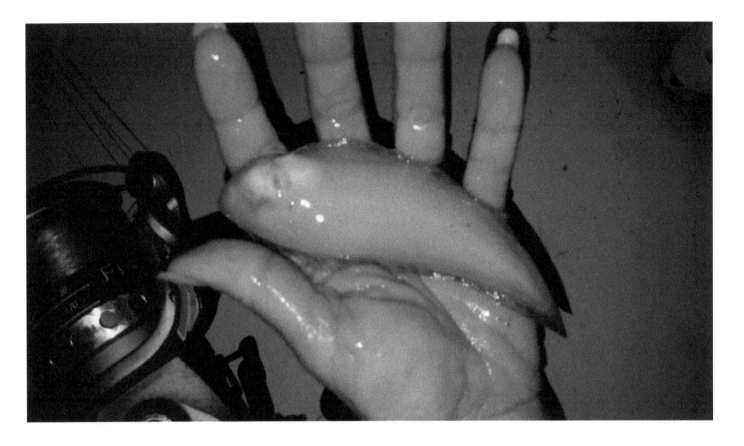

Mike also occasionally catches baby flounder and sole fish in his cast net. They are both in the flat-fish family. The top photo on the opposite page is of a flounder. Both the picture under the flounder and the one above are of sole fish. When flatfish are larvae, they have an eye on each side of their bodies, but as they grow through the juvenile stage, one eye "travels" to the "top" side so that they end up with two eyes on only one side of their bodies, but their mouths stay in the same place.

If you look carefully, you can see the subtle differences between them. Even though they are about the same size, the flounder has bigger eyes and a more fanned tail fin. The sole fish has a more tapered tail. But I think their mouths differ the most. The sole fish looks as if its mouth opening is oval or has a hole in it that prevents it from completely closing. The flounder just has a straight cut for a mouth. The picture above shows the underside or bottom of the sole fish.

CHRISTINE J. RELLI-KUNZ

SALTWATER SWEETIES

One of my favorite fish—not to eat, but to play with—is the sea robin. We have caught these both in Mike's cast net and with our fishing poles. The top picture on the opposite page is a sea robin about the size of my hand. It has both front "legs," which it uses to "walk" along the sea bottom and to sift through sand for food, and "wings," which it uses to "fly" through the water! They have iridescent blue eyes, and their head is shaped almost like that of a frog. When I saw a sea robin for the first time, I was afraid to touch it. Sea robins actually have a mild poison in the spines of their gill plates and dorsal fins.

There were no fishing regulations on sea robins in Florida when we first started catching them. We had a 150-gallon saltwater fish tank at home at the time, so we tried keeping a couple of sea robins in it. But that didn't work out too well. There was a small hole in the top of the tank for the filtration tubes; the sea robins were able to squeeze through and plop down to the kitchen floor. We would be awakened during the night by splashing and croaking. Yup, they croak like frogs too!

The fish pictured below the sea robin is a lane snapper. Lane snappers have a large black spot on their backs; it gets darker if they are threatened and serves as a false eye. This is a common phenomenon with smaller fish. Evidently, larger fish will attack the snapper's tail, thinking it's the head, giving the snapper a better chance of escaping.

The fish pictured above is a sand perch, also known as a squirrelfish. We regularly find these in our traps or catch them when bottom fishing in water at least eight feet deep. Though it's hard to tell from this picture, they have electric-blue, horizontal lines that run the length of their bodies.

CHRISTINE J. RELLI-KUNZ

Occasionally we find seahorses on our crab-trap ropes. Mike also catches many in his cast net, especially when he throws on the grass flats. Some of the ones he catches are so tiny that they're no bigger than the nail on my pinkie finger. There are only two species of seahorses common to Southwest Florida—the lined seahorse and the dwarf seahorse. The dwarf seahorse grows to only about two inches, while the lined seahorse can grow up to eight inches.

The seahorses pictured on the opposite page are lined seahorses. What is really special about the seahorse pictured in the top photo is that it is pregnant—and it's a male! The female transfers her fertilized eggs to the male's pouch, who then incubates them until they hatch. This is the only pregnant seahorse we have ever come across. The pictures underneath the pregnant seahorse show seahorses that are not pregnant, so you can see the difference. It's hard to believe that seahorses are actually considered a type of fish!

The photo above shows a fish we have yet to identify. We believe it could belong to either the goby or mudminnow species. We have found two of these in our crab traps over the years. It has a very soft, slippery skin, but isn't slimy or yucky like a saltwater catfish. I love its white spots—it almost looks as if it has been snowed on!

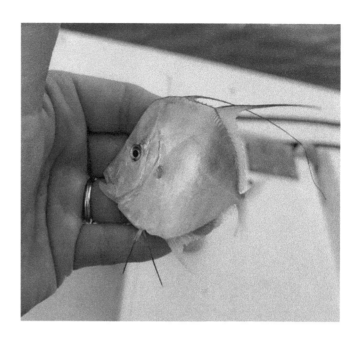

CHRISTINE J. RELLI-KUNZ

Would you believe the lookdowns or moonfish pictured on the opposite page are less than one-half inch thick? Their thinness allows them to move in a flash, and when you look at them head-on, they're virtually invisible. Their body is also extremely reflective. So, when there are a lot of them in a tight school, they can give the appearance of being a single big fish, or blind their predators with their ability to reflect light off their bodies!

The first picture above is a juvenile pompano. Pompano only grow to about twenty-five inches long and look very much like their cousin, the permit, but permit grow twice as big. Many fishermen target adult pompano for their uniquely textured, tasty meat.

The fish pictured below the pompano is a juvenile permit. Unlike pompano, permit are not really known so much for their meat as they are for being a great fighting sport fish.

36 CHRISTINE J. RELLI-KUNZ

The top picture on the opposite page is of a juvenile boxfish. We found this little guy swimming on top of the water a mile or so offshore and scooped him up in our bait net. The second fish pictured is a cowfish. Cowfish are a type of boxfish, their distinguishing feature being the "horns" above the eyes; typically, other boxfish don't have this characteristic.

The top picture above shows a juvenile spadefish. These guys are commonly referred to as our local angelfish. They can get to be about five or so pounds, and their main body can grow larger than a big serving platter.

The picture below the spadefish is a porkfish. Despite finding this guy in one of our crab traps, we primarily catch them around bridge pilings while using a fishing pole baited with small pieces of shrimp. I have no idea why they are called porkfish because I don't think they look much like a pig!

CHRISTINE J. RELLI-KUNZ

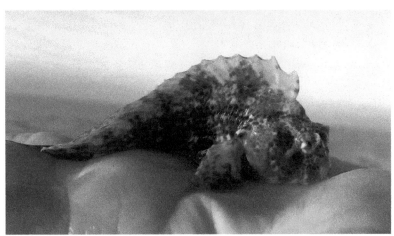

The two fish pictured on the opposite page are a type of puffer fish. They're called striped burrfish. I had to hold the bottom one in place for the picture, or he would have rolled away. We don't know why the top burrfish has a hole in its head in front of its pectoral fin. The top fish pictured above is a Southern puffer; they get much larger than the striped burrfish. Both are common in the waters of Southwest Florida.

When puffer fish become agitated or afraid, they inhale a huge gulp of water to swell their bodies, not only so that they look bigger, but also to make it more difficult for other fish to swallow them. Because puffer fish are usually inflated when they come out of Mike's net, they end up rolling all over the boat like a ball! When released, it may take several minutes for them to return to their normal size, so we have to protect them from any predators, including birds, until they completely deflate and are able to swim.

Puffer fish are very entertaining. These guys can be very vocal, uttering croak-like sounds and noisily spitting water. In my opinion, blowfish, another name for puffer fish, are among the happiest fish in the sea. No matter what subspecies, they always seem to be smiling. When Mike catches one in his cast net, I tell him he caught a smiley.

The second picture above is of a Florida blenny. We've also come across several of these in our crab traps, and all were about the same size; they only grow to about four inches long.

CHRISTINE J. RELLI-KUNZ

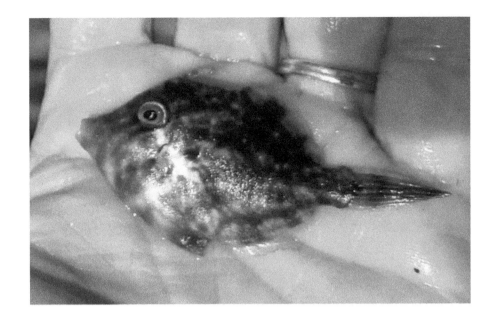

The fish pictured in the top photograph on the opposite page is a white spotted filefish. Mike scooped it up in a bait net while it was hanging out under a crab trap buoy off Fort Myers Beach. This is the only filefish we've ever seen that looks like this. While most white-spotted filefish have easily recognizable and pronounced white spots, similar to those on the fish pictured, many are splotchy or marbled and can be very difficult to identify.

The fish pictured below the white spotted filefish and at the top of this page are of more common filefish, the first being a planehead filefish and the second a common filefish. Mike frequently catches them in his net when throwing on the grass flats of Estero Bay.

The second picture above is of a juvenile jack crevalle. For some reason, its top jaw is only half the size it should be. Its upper and lower jaws should equally meet; however, its condition didn't seem to affect its appetite! A full-grown jack crevalle is pictured in the "Fierce Fighters" section.

CHRISTINE J. RELLI-KUNZ

The top picture on the opposite page is a jackknife fish. Its markings and fins are so cool! The fish pictured below the jackknife fish is a cubbyu fish. These two fish are the only ones of their species we have found in our crab traps.

The fish pictured under the cubbyu fish is a juvenile redfish, which Mike caught in his cast net. Young redfish are referred to as rat reds, but this baby is even too young to be considered a rat red!

At first glance, the two fish above may look similar, but they are two entirely different species. The first one is a juvenile whiting. Mike often catches these in his cast net when he throws on the beach shallows. They live along the shoreline for protection until they mature.

Pictured under the whiting is a juvenile bonefish! In the past thirty years, Mike has caught only five of these babies in his cast net. What's more amazing, is that we have never heard of anyone else catching bonefish in this area. They usually don't swim any farther north than the Ten Thousand Islands, maybe up to Fort Lauderdale on the East Coast of Florida. They are most commonly targeted and caught in the Florida Keys and the Bahamas.

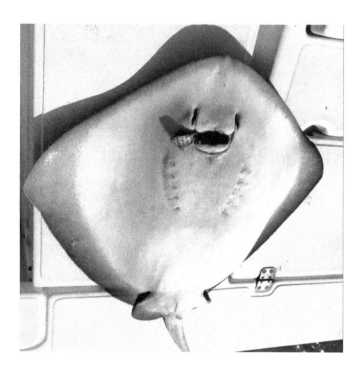

CHRISTINE J. RELLI-KUNZ

THE FIERCE FIGHTERS

The top two photographs on the opposite page show the top side of a cow-nosed ray on the left and either an Atlantic or a Southern stingray on the right. The Atlantic and Southern stingrays look very similar, so it's hard for me to tell the difference from the photograph. My brother, Robert Fox, caught this one, but he graciously let his son, my nephew Taner, hold it up. This was the first stingray Rob ever caught, and he was very proud of it.

The cow-nosed ray is a cousin to the stingray, but it is more closely related to the spotted eagle ray, which is pictured later in this book. While most stingrays prefer to roam the waters of Southwest Florida alone, the cow-nosed ray is a social animal and prefers to travel in groups or "fevers," which can number into the hundreds or even thousands. Notice how their heads and fins differ from the stingrays.

Protruding from the base of their tails, stingrays and cow-nosed rays both have long, venomous spines that can cause extreme pain. Usually, stingray attacks happen when they are startled by being stepped on. That's why it is recommended to do what is called the "Florida shuffle" when in shallow water. Shuffling or dragging your feet in the sand can warn rays of impending danger and give them a chance to swim away. They would much rather do that than be confrontational. However, they have no problem defending themselves when they feel threatened…and stepping on a stingray certainly threatens it.

Many years ago while he was throwing his cast net on a beach in Naples, Mike accidentally stepped on a stingray and was stung just below his ankle. He was in incredible pain from the sting, but it was the beginning of the fishing day. So he suffered for an hour before he couldn't take the pain any longer. We packed up our ten-foot johnboat, carried it over the beach to our van in the parking lot, and went home.

When I called an emergency clinic, they told me the best thing to do was immerse the wound in water as hot as Mike could stand it until the venom was neutralized, keep the wound clean, and apply antibiotic cream until it healed. If you are allergic to stingray venom, or if the stinger breaks off and is still in your body, don't remove it. Go to the hospital immediately! It took nearly six months for Mike's wound to heal completely because the venom actually killed a portion of Mike's flesh. A piece about the size of a nickel fell off, leaving a divot in his foot!

One of my most favorite experiences with cow-nosed rays happened when we were beach fishing on Bonita Beach. While Mike was swimming, he called out and asked me to join him. I asked him why as I was walking in the water, and he said, "Do you trust me?" Of course I did, so I approached him. Mike told me to remain calm and not to make any sudden movements. He then took my hand and led me into water a little deeper than our waists.

Before I knew it, we were in the middle of a fever of hundreds of cow-nosed rays. Some of them barely brushed my skin, or maybe what I felt was just the movement of the water as they swam so near. But I wasn't afraid. It was one of the most amazing experiences I've ever had.

The left picture on the opposite page is of a king mackerel—another fish you do not want to hold by the mouth because they have razor-sharp teeth. I caught him a couple of miles off Bonita Beach. The fish to the right of the king mackerel is one that we catch quite often—a jack crevalle. They are extremely hard fighters. This fight was nearly thirty minutes long, in and out of mangroves and around no-wake buoys. I caught this fourteen-pound bad boy on twelve-pound test using my small rig.

There are four species of fish that comprise the Southwest Florida Backwater Flats Slam and Grand Slam. They are the tarpon, snook, redfish, and spotted sea trout. A Slam is catching one of at least three of them in the same fishing trip, and a Grand Slam is catching one of all four species in the same trip. Mike and I aspire to catching a Grand Slam almost every time we go fishing. But the tarpon only migrate through this area twice a year, in the spring and late summer/early fall. So our chances of getting a Grand Slam are limited to those seasons, but that doesn't stop us from trying all year long!

The bottom picture on the opposite page is a spotted sea trout. It is the smallest of the four species described above. This particular trout was about twenty seven inches, which is considered a "Gator" trout for this area. In fact, with a fish this size, I won a trophy for the largest spotted sea trout in the Adult Open Division of the Gene Doyle Fishing Tournament in 2011. However, trout caught in areas of North Florida, Louisiana, and Texas get much larger than those caught in Southwest Florida.

The picture above is of a juvenile spotted sea trout that we occasionally catch in our cast nets. Most of the trout's teeth are very small, but on their upper and lower jaws they do have two fang-like teeth that leave clean holes in the bait. So, if we miss setting our hook and the bait has two punctures in it, like a vampire's bite, we know we had a trout on the line. It's as if they leave a calling card!

CHRISTINE J. RELLI-KUNZ

The redfish or red drum is one of the most popular sport fish in Southwest Florida. In the 1970s, redfish were on the verge of disappearing from the Gulf of Mexico and possibly headed toward total extinction. However, they are one of the lucky species of fish that have made a miraculous comeback due to federal and state conservation efforts.

The first picture on the left is Mike's biggest redfish; it was about forty inches long. Also pictured is my nephew, Taner Fox, with his very first redfish. He nearly ate the whole thing all by himself!

The redfish's most distinctive feature is its black spots, mostly close to the tail. While most redfish have one spot, some may have none, and some may have two, three, four, or more of various shapes and sizes. In fact, some redfish have so many covering their body that they are referred to as leopard reds.

The redfish pictured above is the closest we have come to catching a leopard red. Because the spots on many redfish are so distinctive, Mike and I have been able to definitively identify having caught the same fish twice in the same weekend, and another twice in one month!

The fish below our leopard red is a black drum, a cousin of the redfish.

CHRISTINE J. RELLI-KUNZ

Snook are among the most coveted sport fish in Southwest Florida. The two snook that Mike and I are holding are females, and the snook Taner is holding—his first one, by the way—is a male. We know this because, like many other species of fish, they are born males. As they mature, they transform into females. Snook and tarpon are among the few sport fish you can actually grab by their jaws. Their mouths may feel like sandpaper, but they do not have teeth.

Another neat feature about snook is their pronounced lateral lines. Almost all fish have lateral lines that run from their gill plates, along their bodies, to the end of their tails. But with snook, it looks as if someone took a magic marker and highlighted their lateral line. Fish use their lateral lines to "see," "hear," and "feel" their surroundings through the vibrations in the water.

The snook I am holding put up a great battle, and both of us were exhausted. So Mike handled the process of reviving the snook after the fight. But while he was flushing fresh seawater through its gills, holding it alongside the boat, a dolphin appeared from underneath our boat and grabbed the snook right out of Mike's hands! The dolphin flung my snook in the air within feet of our boat. Even though we were in about twelve feet of water, it was so clear we could see my snook lying on the sea bottom, belly up.

Mike yelled out, "Not on my watch!" He pulled off his shirt, dove in the water, and scooped the snook up off the bottom. He swam to the boat with it and grabbed on while I used the trolling motor to steer the boat to shallow water. Mike then walked toward shore and released the snook in a shallow creek in the mangroves.

There was a charter captain nearby who had witnessed the fish fight, dolphin attack, and Mike's heroic rescue. We both tried to keep our vessels between Mike and the dolphin, but it got past us and charged Mike. So Mike did what any protector would do—he charged right back at the dolphin!

I videotaped the whole dramatic episode and have included a couple of still shots from that video. Thanks to Mike, my snook lived to see another day!

CHRISTINE J. RELLI-KUNZ

Tarpon, or silver kings, are the most sought-after sport fish in Southwest Florida. They are one of the hardest fighting and most acrobatic fish you can have on the end of your line. They are known for their spectacular jumps and aerial displays when hooked. Mike's longest fight was with a 180-pounder for over four hours—and the fish still wasn't ready to give up. It made one last run right as Mike grabbed the leader—which is considered an official land—before it broke the line. His hands and arms cramped and knotted so badly I had to massage them for thirty minutes before his muscles relaxed.

One of the pointers charter captains give their clients when they've hooked a tarpon is to "bow to the king." This means to lower the tip of your fishing pole to increase the chances your line won't break from the impact of the fish if it lands on your line after a jump.

My most memorable tarpon photo is what I refer to as my "pooping tarpon." If a fish ever photobombed a picture, this one did. I learned a valuable lesson that day—don't squeeze a fish's lower belly!

CHRISTINE J. RELLI-KUNZ

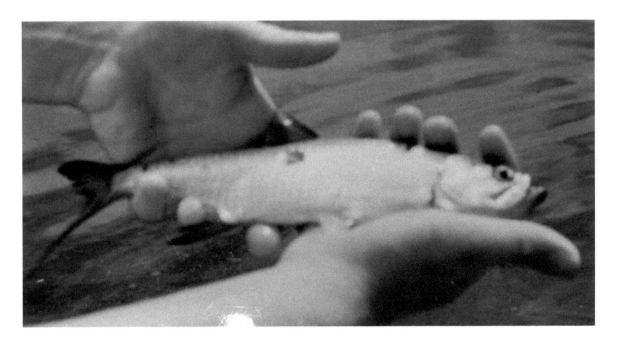

Tarpon can provide the hardest, longest fight any angler could possibly wish for. They have the heart of a champion and the endurance of a bull. The top picture shows about a ninety- or one-hundred-pound tarpon swimming away from the boat after we released it.

The most unique feature of the tarpon is their "whip." They have a small but tall dorsal fin which tapers into a long whiplike appendage that stretches to their tails. If you look closely at the photo of my pooping tarpon, you can see its whip.

While in Collier-Seminole State Park in 1995, Mike cast-netted the smallest tarpon we have ever seen; it is pictured above.

Tripletail, pictured on the opposite page, are my favorite local fish to eat. But they really look weird—almost like prehistoric fish. You have to be very careful handling them because they have razor-sharp barbs on their dorsal fins, anal fins, and gill plates. Tripletail get their name from the elongated shape of their dorsal and anal fins, which give them the appearance of having three tails.

What's really neat about tripletail is that they like to hang out under any kind of floating structure, seaweed, and, especially, crab-trap buoys. We've heard of some fishermen just using their bait or dip nets to catch these guys. Apparently, tripletail think they're safe or invisible when swimming under structures, so they don't scare very easily—unfortunately for them.

Once, we saw a nice tripletail under a buoy, so we stopped and both casted at it. It swam down deeper, until we couldn't see it anymore. Apparently, it ate both our baits before we could feel it on our lines, and we ended up reeling the SAME fish to the boat! Now, that's a "hog fish."

One of the pictures shows what tripletail look like hanging out underneath a buoy. This guy was a couple of feet down the rope, but most of the time we see them right under or next to the buoy.

Juvenile tripletail are a blotchy yellowish and brownish color, which enables them to mix in with floating mangrove leaves as perfect camouflage. They remain in the mangrove estuaries until they reach a size large enough to swim in the open water.

The first picture above is that of a gag grouper which I caught on an artificial reef a couple of miles off Bonita Beach. We don't target reef fish very much, but it was a nice change of pace. The fish on the right is a goliath grouper. This one is not so goliath-looking, but the adults can grow up to eight feet long and weigh as much as 800 pounds!

Pictured on the opposite page are Mike's and my flounders. Notice the difference in color between the two fish. These were caught in Hickory Pass and Lover's Key State Park. A juvenile flounder the size of my hand was pictured earlier in the "Saltwater Sweeties" section of this book.

The fish pictured below the flounders is a cobia or, as Mike likes to refer to them, a "brown clown." He calls them that not just because of their brown color, but because their fight is completely unpredictable. They fight like a bull, swimming everywhere around the boat, including wrapping the fishing line around our motor. And they arbitrarily turn directions on a dime, going in completely opposite directions in a split second. Cobia also happen to be very tasty fish!

The fish pictured above is a bonito, which are in the tuna family. It may be difficult to see from the photo, but they have very pretty squiggly lines on their upper backs. Bonito are caught in Southwest Florida during winter and early spring.

There are many sharks found in the waters of Southwest Florida. The most common are the great hammerhead, scalloped hammerhead, bull, blacktip, spinner, lemon, sharp-nosed, and bonnethead sharks. We have had the pleasure of catching each of these species over the past thirty years.

The first picture on the opposite page is a scalloped hammerhead shark. This one was about six feet long, but they can reach up to twelve feet in length. The great hammerhead shark, which is not pictured, can grow up to twenty feet long and have been known to bite a 150-pound tarpon in half! There is a world-famous professional tarpon fishing tournament that happens every spring in Boca Grande, Florida. Not only do tarpon attract the fishermen, but they also attract the largest concentration of hammerhead sharks in the Gulf of Mexico.

The bottom picture on the opposite page is of a lemon shark. They can reach ten feet in length, but this one is about seven feet long. The pictures above are of a blacktip shark. It's pretty obvious why it's called a blacktip shark—most of its fins are tipped with black. We're not sure, but we think the baby shark, also called a pup, on the next page is a blacktip shark.

CHRISTINE J. RELLI-KUNZ

Our most memorable experience with a shark was one that didn't even involve a fishing pole. One spring several years ago, we were fishing for tarpon in a popular spot a couple of miles off Sanibel Island when we started hearing the fishermen on other boats shouting and pointing at the water. We were a few hundred yards or so from where the commotion started, but whatever was causing it was swimming by a number of boats and getting closer to us.

Then we saw it. It was a huge great hammerhead shark. It slowly swam right up to our boat, and its hammer-shaped head practically touched our boat head-on. It slowly turned and moved alongside us. We were on a sixteen-foot boat, and that shark was as long as our boat!

The pictures on the bottom left are of bonnethead sharks. The bonnethead shark is the smallest species of shark in this area. They grow to three or four feet, at the most, and live primarily on the flats and in the backwater.

Pictured above is a nurse shark. They are one of the most docile local shark species.

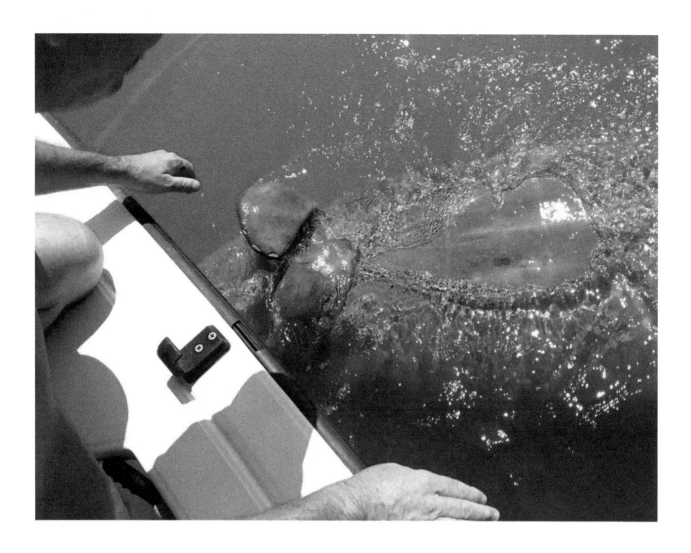

CHRISTINE J. RELLI-KUNZ

THE GENTLE GIANTS

The pictures on the opposite page show our most memorable experience with the friendliest manatee we have ever encountered. It hung around our boat for about thirty minutes while we videotaped it swimming alongside, under, and all around us. We believe this manatee had no fear of us, most likely because it was a rehabilitated manatee and was used to humans. They don't usually hang out like this one did. Though, sometimes, during the heat of summer when we are trolling on the grass flats, manatee will follow us, seemingly enjoying the fanning action of the trolling motor, which feels much like the effect of an air conditioner in the water! The manatee pictured above was covered in algae. It was probably hoping for a good scratch, but despite their friendliness, you are never supposed to touch a manatee.

The top picture on the following page shows one of the many times we have come across a mother and baby in our travels. Actually, she may have had two babies—there was another one following them.

A really cool fact about manatee is that they are a distant cousin to the elephant. If you look closely at the manatee's flippers, you can see its nails, or toes. Aside from their basic body shape, those nails are one of the most visible remnants of their common heritage.

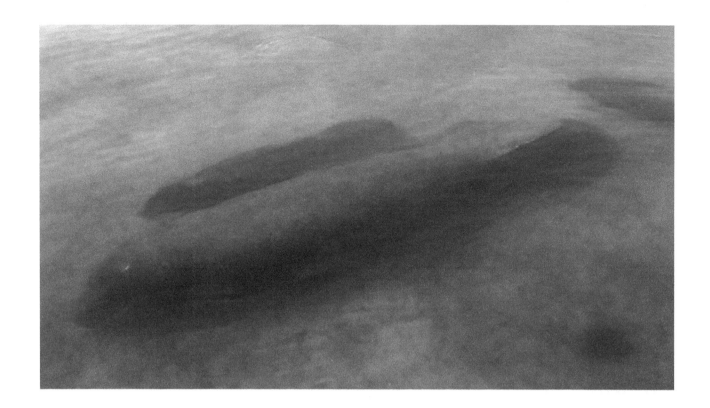

Another of my favorite pictures is of two spotted eagle rays we came across in the Gulf. These rays were more than eight feet across, from wing tip to wing tip—wider than the beam of our boat! We have seen hundreds of spotted eagle rays of all sizes, from juveniles swimming by to adults jumping six feet or more in the air. But this is the only picture I've been able to take of full-grown adults.

In 2020, Mike and I were riding through the minimum-wake zone in New Pass Bay when a juvenile spotted eagle ray with about a three-and-a-half-foot wingspan jumped out of the water, landed on the bow of our boat, slid down the gunwale on my side, slapped me with one of its wings, and slid off the back of the boat, flapping its wings and making squishy noises the whole time!

I actually screamed while trying to get out of its way, making quite a scene for the other boaters' amusement. My initial reaction, of course, was to move out of the way; then my inner fisherwoman urged me to grab it. But finally my voice of reason said, "Really? You want to get speared or stung?" That entire conversation with myself and the actual experience with the ray lasted about two seconds, but it seemed as if it happened in slow motion and lasted for minutes, not seconds. I can still feel when its wet wing hit my arm and side.

Another marine favorite of boaters is the bottlenose dolphin. Most people see them performing in shows at aquatic-themed parks. But to see them free jumping and playing in the wild is so much more exciting. The photo above is from when we came across a pod of dolphin numbering in the dozens, many jumping and playing all around our boat.

If you're lucky, sometimes you can coax dolphin to swim and jump in the wake of your boat. The momentum of the wake makes swimming almost effortless for the dolphin. There is an area by Big Carlos Bridge, at the south end of Fort Myers Beach, where dolphin frequently congregate and show off for the amusement of many boaters.

CHRISTINE J. RELLI-KUNZ

OUR FEATHERED FRIENDS

This is the first and only flamingo we have ever come across in the wild in the thirty years we've been fishing in the Southwest Florida area. But a charter captain we know remembers seeing a small group of flamingos in the Estero area around 1990. Until the 1800s, flamingos were known to migrate to South Florida from Cuba, the Yucatan, and the Bahamas. However, overhunting for their feathers nearly wiped them out in Florida.

Even though flamingos have not traditionally been considered native to Florida, there seems to be mounting evidence that they may, in fact, be a native species. The Audubon Society and the Nature Conservancy have recently reported wild flocks in Palm Beach County, Florida, and in the Everglades/Ten Thousand Islands area of Florida.

We first saw this flamingo in 2013 on the Estero Bay grass flats. About a month after he first appeared, we last saw him on a sand bar at the southern tip of Lovers Key State Park and took the picture above.

The bottom right photograph on the opposite page is that of a great egret. We see great egret each time we're on the water. But we don't have many pictures of males in full-mating plumage. See the delicate feathers at the end of this egret's tail? Those only appear on males during the mating season. Although not seen in this picture, male great egret also get a patch of neon green coloring around the base of their beaks during the mating season.

The birds in the first photograph on the opposite page are roseate spoonbills. We usually only see these colorful birds first thing in the morning. Notice the flat, spoonlike shape of their bills, or beaks. They move the end of their bills in a side-to-side motion, sifting through sand in shallow water searching for tiny shrimp. Spoonbills get their pink color from eating pink shrimp—even their eyes are pink.

For many years, we saw a flock of spoonbills in the New Pass area where it meets the inland waters of Lovers Key. They were there during the dawn hours, and if Mike didn't look directly at them, they would allow him to get close while he walked the mud and sandbars throwing his cast net. As with many wild animals, if you don't acknowledge their presence by looking in their direction, they will generally go about their business as usual, so long as you don't make a lot of noise. But as soon as you stare at them or try to take their picture, they become alarmed and leave—much to my chagrin.

The other magnificent bird pictured on these two pages is the great blue heron. The one that appears to be running is actually chasing our bait. We were using a six-inch mullet to catch snook under the docks, and this bird would not leave it alone. We eventually had to give up fishing there and move somewhere else because he scared all the snook away!

The photo above is my favorite photo of a great blue heron. See the baby in the nest? Great blue herons build their nests in colonies, which can number into the hundreds. There are a few mangrove islands in Estero Bay, which serve as nesting areas for birds, called rookeries, and are close to where Mike sometimes throws his cast net for bait. Just as the sun's first faint glow starts to appear on the horizon, the babies wake up and start crying for food. In the still of the morning, you can hear the babies' cries from these islands several hundred yards away, and the sound gets almost deafening the closer you get to them.

CHRISTINE J. RELLI-KUNZ

Pictured on the opposite page is a very photogenic little blue heron. This guy really wanted to show his best poses for the camera! Little blue heron only grow to about half the size of the great blue heron.

Pictured above is the majestic yellow-crowned night heron. This bird is easily identified by the white streaks on the side of its head and the crest feathers on top of it. Unfortunately, we don't see very many of these beautiful birds.

CHRISTINE J. RELLI-KUNZ

The bald eagle is truly one of the most regal and majestic birds in Southwest Florida. Unlike ospreys, which are a common sight in the backwater and shoreline areas, we don't often see bald eagles. Though he wasn't happy about it, this eagle was very cooperative in posing for his picture. That is because eagles and ospreys don't get along very well, and it thought there was an osprey nearby. Mike learned some time ago how to imitate the call of the ospreys. While I was taking this picture, that's what Mike was doing; and it startled the eagle.

The other photo of a bald eagle shows how bulky their legs look due to their feathers. Seeing it, Mike exclaimed, "He's got his pants on!"

There is another type of eagle we've come across, but only a few times—the golden eagle. Unfortunately, we don't have a picture of one, but imagine a bird twice the size of a bald eagle! Many years ago, a golden eagle built a nest in the top of a Florida pine tree near the south end of Big Hickory Island. Its nest was about six to seven feet across!

The birds pictured above are white pelican. They are much larger than their cousin, the common brown pelican. They can reach over five feet in height when stretching their necks and bills, and they have a wingspan averaging over eight feet. We usually see them in the Estero Bay area during the winter season, but there is a flock or two that reside in the J. N. "Ding" Darling National Wildlife Refuge on Sanibel Island year-round. We occasionally see them on oyster and sandbars or flying in a V formation very high in the sky. Just like the pink flamingo, the wings of the white pelican are etched in black as if they were dipped in black paint.

CHRISTINE J. RELLI-KUNZ

Pictured on the opposite page is a Wilson's plover. They are usually seen on the shoreline, searching for tasty morsels in the sand while chasing the waves as the water retreats back into the sea. What was unique about this particular plover was that it was missing a foot. It may have even been missing a third toe on its good foot. I spent several minutes watching this plover, feeling sorry for it at first.

Even though it had a limp, it was soon apparent its handicap didn't seem to interfere much with its appetite or ability to hunt. I took a picture of its tracks—you can see the pattern of one footprint… then a hole…one footprint…then a hole.

The bird pictured above is an anhinga, or more commonly referred to as a snakebird because it frequently swims with only its neck and head above water—just like a snake. Anhinga are commonly mistaken for cormorants, but you can most easily tell them apart by the shape of their beaks. Anhinga have a straight, daggerlike beak; cormorants have a curved beak.

This bird was drying its wings after diving for food. We happened to see him at the mouth of Big Hickory Pass in 2007. After developing the photo from thirty-five-millimeter film, we loved the picture so much that Mike had it blown up to eighteen-by-twenty-four inches and framed. It is still hanging in my office at work today.

The ospreys shown on the opposite page belong to the hawk family and are the most common raptors found near water in this area. As indicated earlier, ospreys are formidable opponents of the bald eagle and are superb hunters. We see ospreys diving on mullet almost every weekend. Sometimes it appears the mullet being carried off by an osprey weigh twice as much as the bird itself! We have even seen osprey drop their fish or not even be able to lift them out of the water because the fish they have grabbed are so large.

The second osprey pictured was one that grabbed a mullet from the end of my hook. Despite my best efforts to reel my bait in as quickly as possible, it came from behind me and grabbed my bait. When that happens, we reel the bird to the boat and wrap a towel around its head to calm it down. This allows us to carefully remove the hook. I'm happy to report this osprey flew away unharmed and healthy…though probably not very happy!

Another species of bird commonly found on beaches and on oyster bars is the American oyster-catcher, which is pictured above. The male is black, brown, and white with a bright-orange or reddish beak. Unfortunately, this photo doesn't show the male's colorful beak very well. The females, on the other hand, are unremarkably brown.

CHRISTINE J. RELLI-KUNZ

OTHER MESMERIZING MOMENTS

The picture of the sea turtle on the opposite page is a Kemp's ridley turtle. Not only is it the smallest sea turtle, but it is the rarest and most endangered sea turtle in the world. However, thankfully, the National Oceanic Atmospheric Administration reports their numbers have been steadily increasing since 1985. We have been privileged to come across several in the Gulf of Mexico over the years.

Soon after Mike and I started dating, we were swimming on Bonita Beach when an adult green sea turtle, the largest sea turtle, came right up to us—it had to have been close to 200 pounds!

We generally use cut mullet as bait for redfish, larger live mullet for tarpon and shark, and smaller live mullet for snook. When we have enough mullet, we're off to look for smaller pilchard and threadfin herring. Mike likes to have several different kinds of bait because, just like humans, not all fish eat the same thing. In the picture on the opposite page, you can see Mike coming back to the boat with a medium-sized mullet in his net, while a great blue heron is hoping he'll drop it!

Even the end of the fishing day is fun. It seems as though most of the birds that regularly hang out at the boat ramp recognize our boat. As we approach the docks, they rush to meet us. Swimming in the water, the pelican usually follow us, and the giant and snowy egret land on our boat—all hoping for a free, easy meal. And we usually have plenty of bait left over to appease them. The snowy egret are smaller versions of the giant egret and are excellent at catching fish in midair. If you look closely at the snowy egret on our poling platform—its wings are spread—you can see a baitfish in its bill.

82 82 CHRISTINE J. RELLI-KUNZ

We have to get out of bed between four-thirty and five in the morning to get to our bait spots before the sun comes up—it take us thirty minutes to drive to the boat ramp. The first thing Mike does is throw a nine- to twelve-foot cast net for mullet, depending on where we are, while I use a spotlight to look for mullet in the dark. If there are any mullet where I shine the light, they startle and jump out of the water. That's how Mike knows where to throw his net. Even though there are no mullet "showing themselves" in the beam of our spotlight pictured to the left, Mike is standing ready with his net on the bow of the boat, just in case.

By the way, this is absolutely my favorite time of the day. The stars, comets, moonsets, and sunrises are breathtaking to watch. We even see the International Space Station and the Hubble telescope in the sky occasionally.

Once, while we were looking for mullet, we startled a huge flock of roosting seagulls at Big Carlos Point. The noise they made was incredible. Mike and I couldn't hear each other, even though we were only a few feet apart, and the seagulls were twenty to thirty yards away. Thank goodness they were that far away, too, because we could have gotten very dirty!

We came across the little alligator pictured above many years ago in Pine Island Sound, just north of Woodrings Point. He was about five feet long. We also once saw another one in the backwaters of Estero Bay. I actually have video of that alligator.

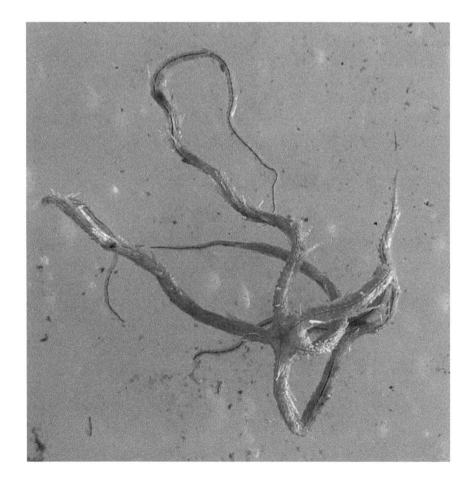

CHRISTINE J. RELLI-KUNZ

Raccoons roaming along the edges of mangrove islands are also a common sight. We saw this raccoon on a mangrove island called Coon Key. We assume it's called Coon Key because there are a lot of raccoons on it! If I shine our spotlight toward the mangrove roots, sometimes we'll see a pair or more of raccoon eyes looking right back at us. But it's so dark all you can see are glowing fluorescent-green eyes!

The starfish pictured to the left is a brittle star. Unfortunately, he was camera shy and would only show his underside!

You've heard of the book *The Cat in the Hat* by Dr. Seuss? Well, above is a photo of the saltwater version—the crab in the hat! We were about two miles offshore when we saw it. The crab was on the front of the hat at first, but I couldn't get my camera out in time to take a good picture, so I've circled it in blue for you.

While I enjoy walking along the shoreline and digging through shell mounds in search of shells to add to my collection, I think I love looking in our crab traps even more. It's like finding hidden treasure. Even if we could keep live shells in Southwest Florida (the laws vary by region), I couldn't bring myself to kill an animal just for its shell. So I study them, play with them, and take lots of pictures.

The top photo on the opposite page shows many of the common shells we come across; these were empty. From left to right, they are the banded tulip, juvenile fighting conchs, apple murex, and olive shells. The center picture shows one of the biggest live banded tulip shells we have ever found in our crab traps; it was as big as my whole hand. Also pictured is a live giant Atlantic cockle shell—look at how speckled the animal is!

The bottom left picture shows several different live shells from our crab traps: the lightning whelk, adult fighting conchs, horse conch, apple murex—which is the smallest one in the center—olive, banded tulip, and several conical spined sea stars. The pictures above show some lightning whelks and what their egg casing looks like. I put my foot in the picture to indicate the size of the casing.

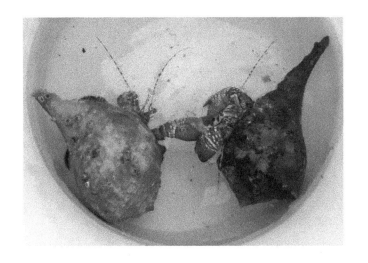

CHRISTINE J. RELLI-KUNZ

The shells in the left picture on the opposite page have been claimed by saltwater hermit crabs. The shells may not be fighting conchs, but they are definitely conchs that are fighting! We found them in one of our crab traps while they were entangled in battle, probably to try out the other's shell for size. They continued their fight when I put them in the bowl, oblivious to the change in their surroundings. I watched and videotaped them for as long as I could before Mike needed me to bait the trap.

The picture to the right of the hermit crabs appears to be a lightning whelk and a fighting conch either fighting or eating each other. Whatever they were doing, they were doing it in very slow motion!

The bottom picture on the opposite page is of a large piece of driftwood that has been decorated with shells by visitors to Lovers Key State Park for years. It seems as though every time the wind, tide, or storms remove the shells, anyone who passes by redecorates the driftwood to keep the tradition alive.

We have seen several SpaceX liftoffs in the predawn hours while on the water. Pictured above is the June 13, 2020, liftoff of a SpaceX Falcon 9 rocket, as seen from Estero Bay, over 200 miles away from Cape Canaveral. It was a spectacular sight!

CHRISTINE J. RELLI-KUNZ

MAJESTIC SKIES

Being on the water during the predawn hours through sunrise is absolutely my most favorite place to be. Have you ever seen the end of a rainbow? If not, you have now. The top pictures on the opposite page are of a double rainbow with the makings of a third rainbow spiking in the middle; these were taken while it was raining. The rainbow actually ended on the water between our boat and the mangroves. This was the first time we had ever seen the end of a rainbow—unfortunately, though, we didn't see a pot of gold!

Underneath the rainbow pictures is one of the most unique rain clouds we've ever seen. It was so low to the ground that you could barely see the sun rising between the cloud and the horizon. There seemed to be a hole or window in the cloud, so you could see the rain falling in the middle of it. But the most unique feature of the cloud was what looked like a shark swimming through it!

CHRISTINE J. RELLI-KUNZ

The top picture on the opposite page shows an iridescent cloud. They usually accompany thunderstorms or rain clouds when sunlight refracts off water droplets in the clouds.

The final pictures are the most unique sunsets we've ever seen, other than those with a green flash. We've seen two green-flash sunsets in the thirty years Mike and I have been together, but we haven't been lucky enough to photograph them.

We refer to the sunset pictured on the opposite page as the "sun-bolt set." At first, we thought the effect was just a lens glare from my camera, but we each took several pictures with two different cameras, and the pictures from both devices showed the same Z-shaped sun bolt on the upper left quadrant.

Everyone sees different shapes in clouds and imagines they look like different objects. To me, the picture above looks like the Offshore Angler marlin logo—think Bass Pro Shops! We can't imagine a more fitting sunset for fishermen and sea-life lovers, especially as the final picture of this book. We have taken pictures of hundreds, if not thousands, of amazing sunrises, sunsets, moonrises, and moonsets—no two are ever alike.

There's nothing that can compare to the feeling of a fish on the end of our lines, the smell of fresh salt air in our lungs, the sound of the waves rolling onshore, and the sounds of the different birds and fish. Yes, fish make different sounds. Schools of glass minnows being crashed by tarpon and snook sound like rain showers; schools of pilchard, also known as greenies or shiners, sound like the light sprinkling of rain; mullet jump and slap their tails on the water; and spotted eagle rays do belly flops. We can tell the difference between the sounds manatee and dolphin make when they exhale, between the trills and calls of bald eagles and ospreys, between the whooshing sounds made by the wings of pelican and seagull—all of this and much, much more we know without even opening our eyes.

Mike and I hope sharing our experiences will help to inspire and nurture the same passion for our local waters and surrounding estuaries, for the importance of conservation, for the thrill of fishing, and for the awe and respect of Mother Nature that we have.

CPSIA information can be obtained
at www.ICGtesting.com
Printed in the USA
BVHW020800290622
639702BV00009B/5